British Values: A Poetry Collection

©2022 Catherine West-McGrath

Published by Parks & Mews 2022

The right of Catherine West-McGrath
as the author of this work
has been asserted by her
in accordance with
the Copyright Designs and Patents Act 1988.
All rights reserved, including
the right of reproduction
in whole or part in any form.

ISBN: 978-1-7391133-0-8

Other poetry collections
from Catherine West-McGrath:

Homesick for the North and Other Poetry

Lapsed Capitalist: A Poetry Collection

Optimistic Activist: Poetry and Verse

What She Really Means and Other Poetry

Try This, It Might Help: Poetry and Verse

The Poems and Lyrics

British Values 1
Bullingdon Club Britain 2
History Came Back 3
Stages of a Break-Up 4
The Launderette 5
Jubilee 6
Packages 7
The Real Betrayer* 8
Iatrogenic Games 10
The Women's Game 11
Gender Budgeting 12
Look Elsewhere 13
A Life in Politics 14
Good Governance 15
Please Your Momma* 16
Tiny Footsteps 18
The Baron and the Witch 19
What Harm? 20
A Woman Who Speaks 21
Doing All The Right Things 22
Can We Listen?* 23
Literature 26
Woke Psychodrama 27
Purse Strings 28
It Couldn't Happen Here, Could It? 29
Still Standing But Wobbling 30
Humans in Women's Bodies 31
Slow Down* 32
Such Good Parties 33
Fascism Flourishes 34

Cash for Access 35
Hero and Guide 36
Clarendon Schools 37
Populists 38
For Thomas Paine 39
Off the Grid 40
Select Committee 42
Feel Only The Kindness 43
Holocausts 44
Cox's Bazar 45
Human Rights 46
This Patient Needs an Advocate 47
Kondratieff Cycles 48
Tabula Rasa 49
Chartered Flights 50
The Letter 51
Awake 52
Fragile Democracy 53
Without Favour or Fear 54
The Dashboard 55
Who? 56
The Earth Knows 57
The Highway Code 58
Who Benefits? 59
Articles and Protocols 60
Corruption? 61
All The Things We'll Never Do* 63
Doctrine of Necessity 64
Heal and Grow* 65
Backlog Britain 67
Odessa* 68
Never Take Peace for Granted 70

Lyrics

British Values

Consider British values
Let's begin with Democracy
Followed by the Rule of Law
Next Individual Liberty
Not forgetting
Respect and Tolerance
For the stranger and the friend
The values upon which
Our society depends

Bullingdon Club Britain

Bullingdon Club Britain
What larks these misdemeanours
No matter what the damage
We can leave it to the cleaners

Reminders of past parties
When drunk and off their faces
They'd leave behind a trail of vomit
And other such disgraces

Then rolled up notes could be unfurled
To offer compensation
Reminding those who tidied up
To stay below their station

Old members still believing
Their charm and wealth protects them
Now face a growing anger
And a public which rejects them

History Came Back

History came back
We hadn't seen its end
Shifted continents perhaps
To places far enough away
For us to feel its movements

History came back
To see what it had missed
While travelling to distant cities
Seeking art works left to us
By older civilisations

History came back
It had missed our conversations
Now it had some important news
Half excited half weary
I know this land well

Stages of a Break-Up

That one perhaps
But not this one
What is their hesitation?
What did I say?
Why this delay?
I crave an explanation

Perhaps they sleep
Or may be ill
That surely makes more sense
Other demands
I understand
I'm surely not past tense

That gift we shared
Nothing compared
I thought was valued too
But clearly so
They let it go
I watched it smash in two

I pledged they'd not
Be once forgot
That promise now has left
These days I smile
Once in a while
No longer so bereft

The Launderette

The launderette
For kleptocrats
To wash their money clean
When during a flight
An oligarch changes
Into an entrepreneur
Looted assets become
Foreign investment
Corruption only happens
Somewhere else. Right?
The originator
Who wrote the rules
Then couldn't afford it
Anymore
So becomes
The butler
Impeccably dressed
Excellent manners
Discrete
Offers advice
When asked
But always has a role
Whether in its banks
Or law firms
Or accountants
Or estate agents
Or legislature
Where its mansions
And schools
Even its peerage system
Can offer an air
Of respectability

Jubilee

A trumpet
A horn
A message
A celebration
A time for debts
To be cancelled
A time of forgiveness
A time to repair
A time to restore
A time to renew
A time to reset
A Jubilee

Packages

The gifts are brought to the factory gates
Production lines keep turning
Conveyor belts roll faithfully
The gifts must go on learning

They're wrapped in paper dull and brown
And if they pass inspection
Are labelled so appropriately
If not sent for correction

Then scanned they fall into their carts
And sent to buyers markets
Replacing previous gifts worn out
From hours of meeting targets

And if an accident occurs
Where packages are damaged
The factory owner sees to it
The incident is managed

But gifts who run past factory gates
And leave behind their duty
Are free to live their lives in all
Its full authentic beauty

The Real Betrayer

I love, I love, I love
At last I live
x 2

If it pleased you I'd like to show it
Any dance and I'd probably know it
I'd been learning those steps every day
Since I'd learned to be taught
Your next move I'd anticipate it
Your next fall I'd be waiting for it
I'd already imagined responses
But here's what I thought

You called me the real betrayer
But who was the real betrayer?
Just who was the real betrayer?
After all

It was only us two you could hide it
One more thing I could keep it inside if
I would cover for you had no doubt
That I'd be on your side
I was wrong you were right and you told me
That's the way you'd got liking to hold me
I left reason behind I'd a sensitive mind
But that night

You called me the real betrayer
But who was the real betrayer?
Just who was the real betrayer?
After all

The Real Betrayer cont.

From up here I can see
More clear than ever
Those oh so pretty patterns
On the ground
From up here I can see
So very clearly
If only I could tell you
What I've found.

But you called me the real betrayer
Now who was the real betrayer?
Oh just who was the real betrayer?
After all

I love, I love, I love
At last I live
x 2

Iatrogenic Games

Another guest brought
To tonight's party game
But don't welcome them in
Or enquire of their name

And you mustn't explain
What the rules are of play
They will guess who spots who
In a couple of days

When they give you a smile
Just look straight ahead
As they're taking their tray
Back alone to their bed

Too unwell to get washed
Let them stay in their dirt
Haven't eaten all day?
Well it's not going to hurt

When they're trying to sleep
Switch on florescent lights
After days doing nothing
They don't need peaceful nights

If a relative calls
Tell them everything's well
For with games such as these
Who'll believe if they tell?

The Women's Game

At best curious and perhaps amusing
At worst financially abusing
Victorian girls kicking a ball
The most unladylike of all

Should muscles form from fast escape
Their rounded curves risked losing shape
And no sports crowds would be impressed
By females inappropriately dressed

But wartime saw increase in play
Crowds happy then to even pay
The men who played before had gone
Leaving the girls to still play on

Soon afterwards the men returned
The women players quickly learned
Their playing was a threat and so
The FA ruled that they should go

Excluded from the pitch and play
They hoped the game would fade away
But no ban could put out the fire
That fuelled these players' one desire

A century's gone and this formation
Inspires a hopeful waiting nation
Never again will women hear
Their football skills aren't welcome here

Gender Budgeting

How do we spend our money?
The taxes we return
If we take a closer look
Is there something we might learn?

For example, if we choose to spend
Our money on destruction
Does one gender benefit more
Because they've chosen that instruction?

Or if education and caring
Should need the highest share
Might a certain gender gain more
Finding jobs are plenty there?

Asking who our leaders champion
When deciding how they spend
Might allow us to decide who
We might vote for in the end

Look Elsewhere

You ought to be worrying
About other disasters
Say those who believe
They're the citizens' masters
Admonishing media
And public broadcasters
When they wish the agenda
Would move along faster

When their future's not bright
May be facing the dock
Want to focus our minds
On more terror and shock
They point in the directions
They think we should look
The citizens' masters
Oldest trick in the book

A Life in Politics

A constituent requires help
For a problem you might fix
The opposition party
Is up to their old tricks

Reports to read before a vote
To add into the mix
Another day when elected
To a life in politics

Good Governance

Examples of Good Governance
Though these rarely make the news
Participation and Consensus
Bring a different range of views
Accountable and Responsive
The Rule of Law no doubt
Equitable and Inclusive
So no one is left out
Effective and Efficient
In the short time we're allowed
We're merely temporary stewards
Looking after things for now

Please Your Momma

Some romances
Well they take their chances
And they fly before they walk
And they sing before they talk

Some love stories
Only share their glories
And they play love like a game
It's a way to hide the shame

Hey you
Things are different now
And you don't have to do that
No we don't have to do that
It's true
Things are different now
And you don't have to be that
No we don't have to be that

So don't get married
Just to please your momma
You've only known that boy
For a summer
There's so much you have to know
And so far you have to go
No don't get married
Just to please your momma
You've only known that boy
For a summer
There's a life for you to live
And so much you've got to give

Please Your Momma cont.

Wedding dresses
Come with their own stresses
And that pretty sweet bouquet
Will have wilted in a day

Invitations
Lead to situations
Throw a party that's okay
Then you're free to walk away

For you
Things are different now
And you don't have to do that
No we don't have to do that
Think this through
Things are different now
And you don't have to be that
No we don't have to be that

No don't get married
Just to please your momma
No don't get married
Just to please your momma
No don't get married
Just to please your momma
No don't get married
Just to please your momma

Tiny Footsteps

Life's not a bus tour
Stopping off at events
Where in between I can zone out
If I just reach the next stop
Then I'm sure to be happy
That's not what this life is about

But life is my footsteps
And each tiny footstep
Can be taken on purpose with care
And with each tiny footstep
I can choose to be happy
So I'll always be happy somewhere

The Baron and the Witch

Last night I had a dream
In which the Baron and the Witch
Were exiled in a castle
In fact there'd been a switch

Instead a Fairy Godmother
And her two kind-eyed young sons
Had replaced the gruel soaked millet
With sandwiches and buns

No more did children fear the dark
Their hungry faces pale
Or travellers risk capture
And banished to a jail

Now butterflies and bunting
Fluttered free throughout the land
And laughter pealed like church bells
Where misery was banned

What Harm?

What harm
A sandwich in a room?
While funerals
Watched over Zoom
Followed 'Goodbyes'
Heard on the phone
Or via Facetime
Still all alone

We partied on
Hard now to think
We smuggled in
More booze to drink
We worked so hard
Needed a rest
Our team required
Some play at best

And afterwards
All that you did
Was quietly close
The laptop lid

A Woman Who Speaks

A woman who speaks
Is outspoken
A woman with an opinion
Is opinionated
A woman who says 'No'
Is pathetic
A woman who persists
Is a pest
A woman who challenges
Is challenging
A woman who asks 'Why?'
Is belligerent
A woman who questions 'Can't'
Is cantankerous
A woman who uses her power
Is playing power games
A woman who defends herself
Likes confrontation
A woman who questions BS
Is talking BS
A woman who takes up space
Doesn't belong
A woman who thinks
Shouldn't share her thoughts
A woman with a voice
Is every woman

Doing All The Right Things

Through no fault of her own
She did everything right
When she took a walk home
On her last fateful night

But

Did she stay under lights?
Did she use her alarm?
Did she plan out her route?
To avoid any harm

Did she say she'd text friends
When she got to her door?
To say 'Home safe and thanks
So don't worry no more'?

Did she wear modest clothes?
Use a new clever app?
Where a smart satellite
Locates life on a map

Did she fear one last time?
That she wouldn't arrive?
Despite all this she failed
Just to get home alive

Can We Listen?

Deny, deflect, dismiss
Distract, defend, desist
Destroy, delude, delay
Another sigh another day

Ignore, avoid, neglect
Refuse, rebuff, reject
Walk out, upset, undo
Where is the love I shared with you?

But can you listen?
Tell me can you listen?
Tell me can you listen?
Are you listening this time?
But can you listen?
Tell me can you listen?
Tell me can you listen?
Are you listening this time?

Some day soon
You and me we won't be fighting anymore
Fighting anymore
Someday soon
You and me we won't be fighting anymore
But until then will you wait
Till I'm not crying anymore?
Crying anymore
But until then
Will you wait for me?

Can We Listen? cont.

Resolve, repair, replace
Restore, renew, retrace
Reclaim, rebuild, review
Is there a way back for us two?

Reveal, release, redress
Reclaim, recure, reset
Retake, reform, remind
Can love be too lost not to find?

But can I listen?
Ask me can I listen?
Ask me can I listen?
Am I listening this time?
But can I listen?
Ask me can I listen?
Ask me can I listen?
Am I listening this time?

Some day soon
You and me we won't be fighting anymore
Fighting anymore
Someday soon
You and me we won't be fighting anymore
But until then will you wait
Till I'm not crying anymore?
Crying anymore
But until then
Will you wait for me?

Can We Listen? cont.

But can we listen?
Ask us can we listen?
Ask us can we listen?
Are we listening this time?
But can we listen?
Ask us can we listen?
Ask us can we listen?
Are we listening this time?

Literature

Still life in a darkened room
A weighty tome by Harold Bloom
Pleased to have found in mint condition
An early print of that edition

Passing temples to worship God
He'd hurry as he crossed the quad
Protected in those ancient walls
To sit and eat in dining halls

Still trying to read the Western Canon
Distracts so not to self examine
Can literature ever teach us more?
And what are family secrets for?

Another character dissected
Another plot to be inspected
Consider roads that we might take
So not to make the same mistake

The stories stacked upon the shelves
The things they say about ourselves
To be the villain or the guide
Reorders meaning from inside

Woke Psychodrama

The masses are rising
Demanding more justice
This must be reduced and controlled
They speak about fairness
Same rights for minorities
And questioning what they've been told

We must make them frightened
Aware of real enemies
It's better when there's common foes
Otherwise they'll get restless
And if they get restless
They might question what we propose

They must know they're threatened
And we will protect them
They don't have the power to choose
Which stories are loudest
And who gets to tell them
If they know it's a game we might lose

Purse Strings

When deciding which firm
Perhaps we should enquire
Whose interests it lobbied
Before choosing to hire

Declare the donations
Received in return
Might persuade to rethink
There's a lot we might learn

Just who was advised
In return for high fees?
Whose sanctions were fought
When submitting their pleas?

Whose side did they take
When the court was in session?
Perhaps now is the time
We were asking more questions

It Couldn't Happen Here, Could It?

Once given power
They will begin
To further friends careers
But it couldn't happen here
Could it?
No, it couldn't happen here

There's a role for one
In the Upper House
Now another one's a peer
But it couldn't happen here
Could it?
No, it couldn't happen here

Institutions which
Might challenge face
A future full of fear
But it couldn't happen here
Could it?
No, it couldn't happen here

Citizens warned of duties
Now to live a life austere
But it couldn't happen here
Could it?
No, it couldn't happen here

Until no law protects us from
Elite free marketeers
Hope it couldn't happen here
Could it?
Please, it couldn't happen here

Still Standing But Wobbling

Still standing but wobbling
Over serious matters
Past supporters risk seeing
Reputations in tatters
Warned they'll lose their careers
If he should be defeated
So he begs they stay loyal
Till enemies have retreated
There's no one quite like me
I was so good at winning
Wasn't chosen for ethics
And well known for some sinning
Yet they still remain restless
As support is declining
But his plan is for now
That they'll tire of this whining

Humans in Women's Bodies

We are humans in women's bodies
And each day we learn some more
How living in these bodies
Sometimes feels we're in a war

Freedoms we once took for granted
Now we see as under threat
Hoping daughters will know different
But it's just not happened...yet

So we'll keep on elevating
Voices saying we expect
That these humans in women's bodies
Know only freedom and respect

Slow Down

Slow down, come with me
Let's take a walk
Where it's nice to be
Get out of here to
Feel the breeze
Let's find a place to feel
The shelter of the trees

It's all outside waiting
Just for you
There's a world of love
That will get you through

Rest a while
Hear the birds
Hear their song
They don't need no words
Happy to listen
If you've any cares
Tell them your worries
They will never share

It's all outside waiting
Just for you
There's a world of love
That will get you through

You don't have to say a word
That's not necessary
Or you can share what's on your mind
If you've too much to carry
There's a sky outside for you
Big enough for anything you throw
If it weighs too much
Now you can let it go

Such Good Parties

When my friend threw such good parties
Only fair to nominate
For a peerage in our Chamber
Where we work to legislate

When intelligence officials
Warned me of this bad idea
I advised we'd have no bias
Of my party buddies here

Then experts in security
Wished to stop me in my plans
I just stated they were racist
Stopping such unfair demands

Now it looks as if that process
Might be under scrutiny
But we followed due procedure
Interfering? Never me

Fascism Flourishes

Fascism flourishes in moments of anxiety
Groups become targets and named
Labelled the reason a lifestyle is threatened
Doesn't matter which group is to blame

Fascism demolishes equal democracy
When people feel rights might be lost
Leaders remove the ability to be removed
No matter the damage or cost

Fascism isn't studied across the curriculum
Perhaps now's the time it's included
So citizens learn how to spot it much earlier
And electorates can't be deluded

Cash for Access

So is this how it works?
You see your accounts swell
When we give you some cash
We can profit as well?

It's a small contribution
But we get good returns
If at exclusive meetings
You then heed our concerns

So the funds you control
Which the public have paid
Find their way back to us
Once deposits are made

This is worth every pound
Of our generous largesse
When the schemes we design
Are ensured of success

If the press are alarmed
And the public disgusted
Well you never were chosen
For how much you were trusted

Hero and Guide

This is the habit
Of the Hero and Guide
Is curious to know more
Of their treasures inside

Sets an intention
To grow more each day
And always is grateful
For what comes their way

Full of compassion
Accepts life as a gift
Is sure of their purpose
To inspire and uplift

Sees only abundance
Is happy to give
Knows the habit of gratitude
Is the best way to live

Clarendon Schools

The Old Boy network
Knows where it belongs
In seats of power
Influence is strong

It's the way of knowing
A certain confidence
In an order created
From Providence

Though centuries old
No Act can undo
Its prolific status
In the latest Who's Who

Though just nine schools
Still dominate
A nation's thoughts
How it legislates

Until the Curriculum
For the council estates
Includes lessons in rhetoric
And how to win debates

Populists

How does a populist feel
When their popularity has waned?
When the polls detect they're losing
Any voters they once gained?

Where do they go when no longer
Their stories will persuade?
Hoping electorates forget
The falsehoods that were made

When their blame games and distractions
Finally see they're shown the door
And the citizens they used
Ensure they're popular no more

Do they meet up on an island
With their populistic friends?
With the other upset leaders
Licking wounds when their power ends?

For Thomas Paine

Few pamphlets had such
A dramatic effect
Common Sense
Connected with colonists
Whether rich or poor
Writing in plain language
Often scathing
Especially of the monarchy
Describing the Kings of England
As usurpers
Who had stolen power
By force
Because in the beginning
There were certainly
No kings
He asked
When did we choose them?
Or if we were able
To peel back the ages
Would we find their ancestors
To have been the most brutish?
Was that how they became
Leaders of the gang?
And what became of the land
That allowed them to continue?

These were radical words
But they were received well
And so a new order
Of government was created

Today its citizens returned
To celebrate
With the old country's
Subjects outside
The Palace gates

Off the Grid

They lived quite simply on the land
And traded with a few
They tended to their crops just fine
Before the cities grew

Then

They had to be employable
To survive needed a wage
Employers replaced good spouses
In the new industrial age

The three Rs replaced their dowries
Families replaced by schools
Fathers replaced by new patriarchs
Now owners set the rules

They left their homes for factories
The clean air for the smoke
But wealth still was a dream for them
Still found that they were broke

Their descendants still needed to work
Still sought a decent wage
Monitored by technology
In the smart digital age

Now new skills were their dowry
Only for the roles short term
With a boss no longer committed
To a long life with the firm

Off the Grid cont.

But the tech gave them a way out
They could work and stay at home
No, they didn't miss the politics
Found they loved to work alone

Then they didn't need the cities
They could work without the train
And their cars stayed on the driveways
The land was calling them again

So they went back to the country
For a life more off the grid
Tuning back into the seasons
Like their ancestors always did

Select Committee

I'd spied the small room
When taking one of my
Regular walks around
The small garden
Outside the lounge

That's where I'll be
I thought
I will tell them everything
On those soft chairs
In soft light

When I was called to
Meet with you with little notice
I looked forward to that room
But it was not that room
I was led to

Instead a hard light
A hard table and a hard chair
The left table a stenographer
The right table a commentator
Opposite there you were

No one on my right side
No one on my left side
You could have welcomed me
You could have held my hand
You could have sat at my side

Feel Only The Kindness

Kind words
Are like feathers
Dandelion clocks
Faint whispers
Gentle breezes

While insults
Real or imagined
Are like hammers
Swords and
Giants' roars

Holocausts

Holocausts have their beginnings
When human beings are disconnected
A group is seen to cause the ills
To which others are affected

False barriers built to separate
From ourselves and one another
Conditioned to forget how we belong
To only one Earth Mother

Holocausts have their endings
When we end lies and denying
Until then we'll see more cleansing
And unnecessary dying

Cox's Bazar

In the world's largest camp
Tarpaulin and bamboo
Make for vulnerable shelters
Which the flames sweep fast through

In Cox's Bazar
Families are fenced in
Risk of imminent danger
Should a fire begin

In this temporary city
Homes can be quickly lost
And those who lose life
Will pay too high a cost

Precious things few belongings
Are destroyed in a night
Still the camp keeps on expanding
With no ending in sight

Human Rights

Rights for all humans
Can't be taken for granted
Our freedom gets no guarantee
Governments and regimes
Can change in a day
When rights are lost
Quite suddenly

Choices long fought for
In a flash snatched away
When the hand of the clock
Turns an hour
Citizens reminded to still stay alert
And consider who we wish
To take power

This Patient Needs an Advocate

This patient needs an advocate
To navigate this maze
This unfamiliar territory
These labyrinthine ways
But such a right has been denied
This vital voice neglected
Its value not believed by those
Who state it's been rejected

This patient needs an ambulance
Their ailment cannot wait
The hours tick by remorselessly
Until it turns up late
No beds free at the other end
The medics are frustrated
The reasons for such hold ups
And more delays debated

This patient needs a coroner
To seek an answer to
The reason why this life was lost
So justice might win through
The family try to understand
A system decimated
Now need a hearse to say 'Goodbye'
Where life is celebrated

Kondratieff Cycles

Each Kondratieff Cycle
Ends in general crisis
Capitalism must reinvent
Technology drives changes
Turns wheels ever faster
And distances shrink in percent

A trigger brings struggle
New ideas to be tested
Unthinkable previously before
Old models once certain
Are shaken and crumbled
Solutions to problems looked for

These times last for years
While transitions are lived through
And structures must be rearranged
Our houses thought built upon
Solid foundations don't get
Through these crises unchanged

Tabula Rasa

Illegal and unnecessary becomes
Legal and necessary
Scrutiny becomes
Fast-tracked by condensed committee

Law-keeper becomes
Law-breaker
Feeble legal justification becomes
Strong legal justification

In this land
Every day starts anew again
We are in a permanent
State of forgetting

Chartered Flights

There await charter planes
When we need to be flying
Scheduled trips will not do
When there's trade to be buying

Doing business with neighbours
Has been firmly rejected
So long flights see to it
Business miles are collected

Climate goals aren't important
Now we've got it all done
Half a million on journeys
Is essential and fun

Benefits are uncertain
At best meagre returns
Still it's fun to fly private
While below the Earth burns

The Letter

The High Court lets the plane leave
The countdown now begun
And in my hand the letter
Says I'm one of thirty one

Frustrated the UNHCR
Says it never gave endorsement
Despite the Government's false claims
It agreed with this enforcement

This land which opened up its homes
To others fleeing fear
Tells me I have to leave now
I'm just not welcome here

And even when the plane lands
There's still no guarantee
Asylum will be granted
What next will wait for me?

For I'm weary and I'm frightened
I just need a place to rest
Where I'll share my skills and talents
And give only of my best

Future King is disappointed
States appalled at this idea
I just hope appeals are heard and
I can build my new life here

Awake

Awake no thoughts of yesterday
New life new dreams are on their way
Old ways now faded into past
New hope arrived for me at last

An opened door will bring new air
Old clothes no longer wish to wear
Old days now frayed as dirty lace
New sun feels warm upon my face

At threshold of the day I stand
Observe this patch of open land
The grasses left still growing wild
Refreshing breeze the weather mild

Flamingo stand to stem the years
Arms stretched above will skim the ears
Toes touched now hips in loose rotation
To meet the day with fresh elation

Fragile Democracy

This way of life is not won once
And then will always be
But must be nurtured otherwise
Fragile democracy
Can disappear and what we thought
Was ours and here to stay
Is stolen from us suddenly
Because we looked away

Without Favour or Fear

To choose which crime should be looked at
Without favour or fear
Requires a force to act freely
When evidence is clear

To say there isn't quite enough
When photos circulate
May make fair minded citizens
Quite wary of their state

What more must lawyers who seek truth do?
Must they beg and plea?
To ensure that the rule of law
Protects our liberty

For who within this country now
Can this force say it serves?
And can we say our nation has
The justice it deserves?

The Dashboard

How utterly delighted
That we're now able to see
The table of the regs
To be taken soon maybe

For those who like their wine to fizz
They may soon find it shatters
As health and safety rules are ditched
And sense no longer matters

Or those of us who may give birth
Could soon lose out on pay
'Mat rights have now gone just too far'
This Dashboard seems to say

So now we're asked to take a look
At a list meant to protect
And indicate the rights we
Should be happy to reject

But how we wish to see a list
Of ill-thought out decisions
Made in the past by those without
Wise thoughts or certain vision

Who?

Where did these holidays come from?
Who worked so we could rest?

Where did this air come from?
Who breathed so we could breathe?

Where did this representation come from?
Who presented so we could be represented?

Where did this voice come from?
Who spoke so we could speak?

Where did this lesson come from?
Who taught so we could learn?

Where did this power come from?
Who protested so we could protest?

Where did this seat come from?
Who stood so we could stand?

Where did this pen come from?
Who wrote so we could write?

The Earth Knows

Biologists have emphasised
                              But the roots know
The individual
                              But the soil knows
Stressed the contest
                              But the fungi knows
Among discrete species
                              But the phosphorus knows
Selfish genes
                              But the seedling knows
Some scientists advocate
                              But the plant knows
Controversially
                              But the tree knows
A greater focus on co-operation
                              But the forest knows
Over self interest
                              But the Earth knows
Emergent properties
                              But our cells know
Of living systems

The Highway Code

There's some changes occurring
When we're using the road
The Government's updated
The old Highway Code

There's a lot to digest
A new advert is teaching
Like the safe way with doors
Now we're calling 'Dutch Reaching'

Some use roads for fast journeys
Others use just to roam
But if we think of each other
Then we'll all make it home

Who Benefits?

Who benefits from your
Lack of self respect
Shifting balance
To their aims?
Who doesn't mind if
Your sense of their power
Keeps adding
To their gains?

Who benefits if
You think you have
No options
No real choice?
Who hopes you won't
Consider that
You have
A stronger voice?

Who's making sure
It's hard
For you to
Organise a riot?
Who's busy creating
Gossip with
Their stories to keep
You quiet?

Articles and Protocols

We're considering leaving the conversation
To gather with states that prefer isolation
No longer part of the international community
Free to break laws with absolute impunity

Set up after World War Two
A response to fascism and a despotic few
No longer protecting from torture and detention
Churchill was a founder of this Convention

In this game of division and political fights
We're prepared to destroy all of our rights
Out of conversations I try to understand
How I once belonged to an intelligent land

Corruption?

When does corruption at its core
Become a nation's shame?
When do the citizens decide
This won't occur again?

Investigations blocked delayed
Results can be denied
And Chairs selected carefully
Will know which facts to hide

When public cash is handed to
Rich donors who profit
And crises are a perfect cloak
For dealings not legit

No fiscal prudence is required
If deals are done with mates
Only when help for poor households
Is up for more debate

And ruffled hair no longer fools
The voters in the shires
Who've had enough of scandals
And the ones they think are liars

All The Things We'll Never Do

Right there
Right in the middle of nowhere
We were kissing
And the next thing
You walked out
And the door slammed shut

Right there
Right in the middle of a nightmare
You were missing
And the next thing
An explosion
In my gut

And all the things we'll never do
I never got to do with you

Here's the ballroom
Where we'd dance upon the floor all night
Here's the song for you
The song I wrote for your delight
Here's the chauffeur
Who would drive our fancy motorcar
And all the things we'll never do
I never got to do with you

Here's the portrait
We were hanging in the gallery
Here's the writer
Who was gonna write our love story
Here's the tickets
For our first class flights to anywhere
And all the things we'll never do
I never got to do with you

All The Things We'll Never Do cont.

We'd take a rocket ship
Up to the stars each night
We'd make a wish come true
To set our worlds alight
We would stand on the moon
That's what you said we'd do
And all the things we'll never do
I never got to do with you

Doctrine of Necessity

The Doctrine of Necessity
To break Agreements made
Requires such solid arguments
One hopes we can persuade
Through tweets and hurried interviews
Our messages conveyed
No one employing reason could
Be fooled by this charade

Once more we will dismantle
Scaffolds of our reputation
Destroying any structures which
Uphold a lawful nation
While lawyers hang their heads and curse
The news in their frustration
To squeeze out of a mess we made
Entirely our creation

Heal and Grow

Be the change x 5
You wanna see
And then you'll
See the change x 5
That sets you free

Heal and grow x 3
Forget
All you know x 3
It was long ago
But now's the time for
Goodbye
It's worth a try

There's really nothing left to say
That's not been spoken
I'll fix the door
And all the cabinets left broken
I never felt so much alive
And so awoken
As I can feel today
Let's be like grown ups we can end
Without the fighting
I've never found our arguments
All that exciting
If necessary you can put it
All in writing
And we can go on our way

Heal and Grow cont.

Be the change x 5
You wanna see
And then you'll
See the change x 5
That sets you free

Heal and grow x 3
Forget
All you know x 3
It was long ago
But now's the time for
Goodbye
It's worth a try

We're out of talking let's begin
To see some action
Instead of adding let's divide
With our subtraction
We know this formula could do
With some extraction
We've been a terrible mix
My therapist thinks I've been making
Lots of progress
I've told them all the things I thought
I'd never confess
I'll pass their number on they're great when
Love's a big mess
No problem that they can't fix

Backlog Britain

Commissioned reports
Delayed for weeks
So grateful the SpAds
Have stemmed the leaks

Timed for the day
The House will rise
Coincidence
Feign fake surprise

Assure that findings
Are long gone
Although it's clear
Nothing's been done

And why should humans
Tired and weak
Have someone who
They trust to speak?

Whether for those
Who wish to leave
For respite or
Some brief reprieve

Or just the means
To drive away
Yes even those
Will find delay

Odessa

I met you in the music room
One morning in the Spring
You took a simple melody
To make the music sing
In Odessa
And the music still plays over Odessa

You sheltered in the basement
Underneath your favourite bar
Too late to leave the city
But you never would go far
From Odessa
And the music still plays over Odessa

You stopped to sit awhile outside
A house down by the sea
You played a song at sunset
In a soft melodic key
For Odessa
And the music still plays over Odessa

I never learned enough
Or tried to understand
How what we did here made
A difference to your land
Would it have changed at all
The dreams and visions I had planned?
Long ago
So long ago

Odessa cont.

I find the news so hard to watch
Even infrequently
I dream of children playing
On the sand just by the sea
Of Odessa
And the music still plays over Odessa

When dawn comes we'll wake early
And we'll watch the new sun rise
We'll open up our windows
And we'll sing into the skies
Over Odessa
And the music still plays over Odessa
Over Odessa
And the music still plays over Odessa
Over Odessa
And the music still plays over Odessa
Over Odessa
And the music still plays over Odessa

Never Take Peace for Granted

May we never take peace for granted
Never seeking to divide
May we never exploit differences
Forcing people to take sides

May we never label fellow humans
By the place where they were born
Knowing where we're born may at any time
Face disaster, be war torn

May we look for hope in every place
Find only that which will connect
See the family member many times removed
And friends just not met yet

www.ingramcontent.com/pod-product-compliance
Lightning Source LLC
Chambersburg PA
CBHW030044100526
44590CB00011B/326